Space

The Moon

Charlotte Guillain

Heinemann
LIBRARY

www.heinemannlibrary.co.uk
Visit our website to find out more information about Heinemann Library books.

To order:
☎ Phone 44 (0) 1865 888066
▤ Send a fax to 44 (0) 1865 314091
▣ Visit the Heinemann Bookshop at www.heinemannlibrary.co.uk to browse our catalogue and order online.

Heinemann Library is an imprint of Capstone Global Library Limited, a company incorporated in England and Wales having its registered office at 7 Pilgrim Street, London, EC4V 6LB – Registered company number: 6695582

Heinemann is a registered trademark of Pearson Education Limited, under licence to Capstone Global Library Limited

Edited by Siàn Smith, Rebecca Rissman, and Charlotte Guillain
Designed by Joanna Hinton-Malivoire
Picture research by Tracy Cummins and Heather Mauldin
Production by Duncan Gilbert
Originated by Heinemann Library
Printed and bound in China by South China Printing Company Ltd

ISBN 978 0 431 02044 0
13 12 11 10 09
10 9 8 7 6 5 4 3 2 1

British Library Cataloguing in Publication Data
Guillain, Charlotte
  The moon. - (Space)
  1. Moon - Juvenile literature
  I. Title
  523.3

Acknowledgements
We would like to thank the following for permission to reproduce photographs: Alamy pp.**5** (©ImageState), **20** (©Stocktrek Images, Inc.); Getty Images pp. **10** (©Joe Drivas), **11** (©Joel Sartore), **13** (©NASA/Stringer), **19** (©Science Faction/NASA), **22** (©NASA/Stringer), **23a** (©Alamy/ImageState), **23c** (©NASA/Stringer); NASA pp. **9** (©GRIN), **16** (©GRIN/David R. Scott), **17** (©GRIN), **18** (©GRIN/David Scott), **23b** (©GRIN); Photo Researchers Inc pp.**8** (©Science Source/NASA), **12** (©Detlev van Ravenswaay), **21** (©SPL); Photolibrary pp.**4** (©Dennis Lane), **6** (©Corbis); Shutterstock pp.**7** (©Oorka), **15** (©David Scheuber).

Front cover photograph reproduced with permission of NASA (©JPL/USGS). Back cover photograph reproduced with permission of NASA (©GRIN).

Every effort has been made to contact copyright holders of material reproduced in this book. Any omissions will be rectified in subsequent printings if notice is given to the publishers.

Contents

Space

The Moon is in space.

Space is up above the sky.

The Moon

The Moon is a ball of rock.

The Moon is smaller than Earth.

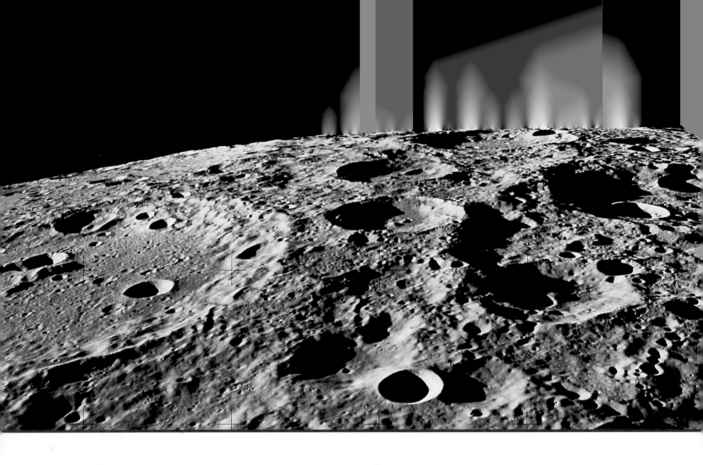

There is no air on the Moon.

There are no living things on
the Moon.

The Moon does not make its
own light.

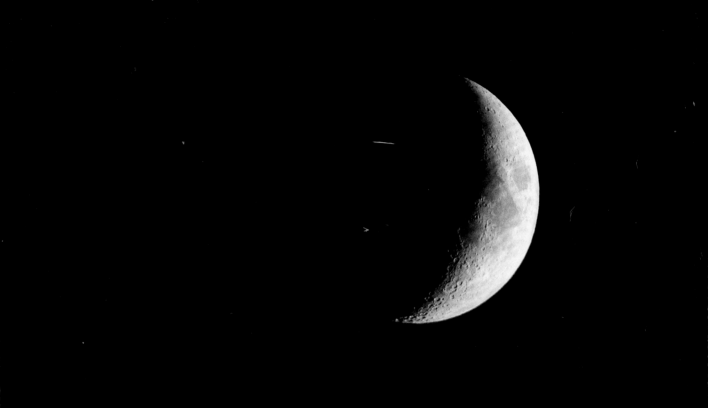

Light from the Sun makes the
Moon shine.

There is dust on the Moon.

crater

There are craters on the Moon.

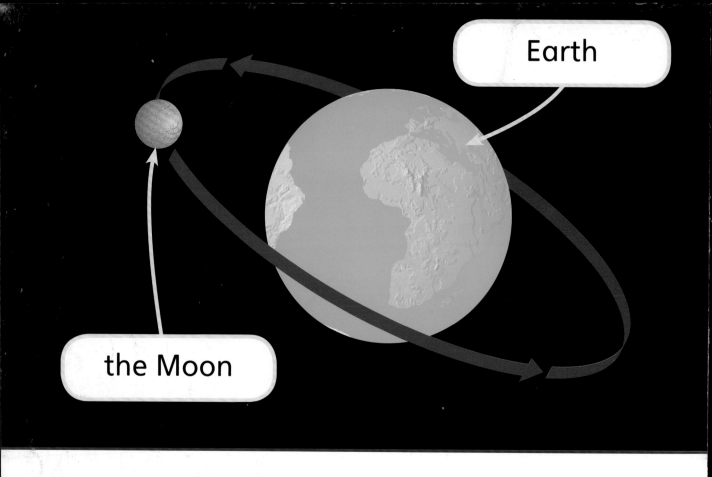

Earth

the Moon

The Moon moves around, or orbits,
Earth.

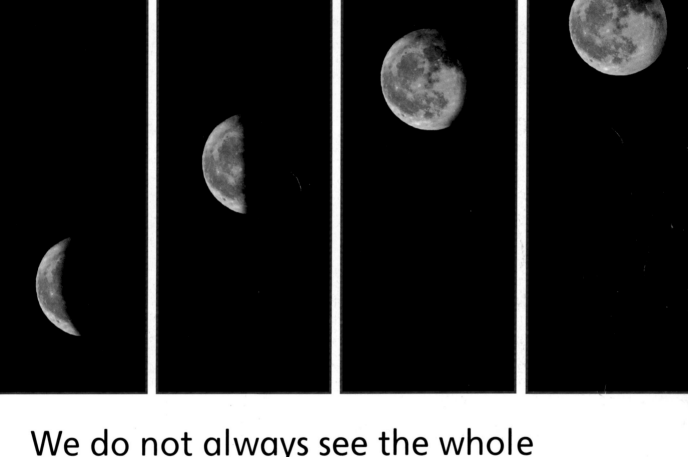

We do not always see the whole Moon as it orbits Earth.

Moon landings

People have visited the Moon.

Astronauts landed on the Moon.

The astronauts collected rocks.

The astronauts looked around
the Moon.

Other moons

There are other moons orbiting other planets.

Some planets have lots of moons.

Can you remember?

What is this?

Answer on p.24

Picture glossary

air we cannot see air but it is all around us on Earth. We need to breathe in air to stay alive.

astronaut person who travels into space

crater hole in the ground, shaped a bit like a bowl

orbit move around

Index

Answer to question on p.22: A crater.

Notes for parents and teachers
Before reading
Ask the children if they have seen the Moon. What shape is it? Does the Moon look the same every time they see it? Have they ever seen the Moon during the day? Explain that the Moon goes round the Earth and that it is smaller than the Earth. The Moon does not make its own light but the light from the Sun makes the Moon shine.

After reading
• Make moon craters. Talk about the craters on the Moon. Explain that craters were made by large rocks crashing onto the surface of the Moon. Place wet plaster of Paris in a shallow dish. Invite the children to drop marbles of different sizes into the wet plaster. Let the plaster dry and talk about how the marbles made dents in the surface of the plaster just as the rocks made the craters in the surface of the Moon.

• Select some "moon music" and encourage the children to mime setting off in a rocket to get to the Moon, landing on the Moon's surface, walking slowly around in their heavy boots, collecting rocks, and returning to Earth.